The Colors Within

A Tool for Caregivers and Professionals Working with Individuals with Dementia

Debbie Merkel, BA, BS, CSW
Photographs by Jayne Marie

Hog Press

Hog Press
PO Box 5069
Madison, WI 53705-5069
USA
hogpress.com
editor@hogpress.com

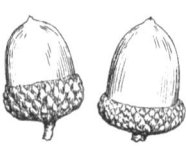

HOG PRESS

THE COLORS WITHIN: A TOOL FOR CAREGIVERS AND PROFESSIONALS WORKING WITH INDIVIDUALS WITH DEMENTIA
Copyright © 2024 by Debbie Merkel, BA, BS, CSW
All rights reserved.

No part of this book may be reproduced in any form by any electronic or mechanised means (including photocopying, recording, or information storage and retrieval) without written permission, except in the case of brief quotations embodied in critical articles and reviews.

For more information, please visit hogpress.com

ISBN: 978-1-941892-95-4

x.com/culicidaepress — facebook.com/culicidaepress
threads.net/culicidaepress — instagram.com/culicidaepress

Our books may be purchased in bulk for promotional, educational, and/or business use. Please contact your local bookseller or the Culicidae Press Sales Department at +1-352-215-7558 or email us at sales@culicidaepress.com

All photos by Jayne Marie © 2024
Design by polytekton.com © 2024

Introduction

It was my fourth week as a Hospice Social Worker. As a Hospice Social Worker, it's my role to help patients and their families with end of life challenges. This includes assessing and anticipating any complex needs, problem-solving and resolving struggles, providing emotional support, and connecting to patients and their families. Although seasoned as a social worker, I was new to working with individuals with Dementia.

The training I received taught me how to talk to someone with dementia. How to communicate. During the past twenty-five years, I received training, and obtained education and experience in working in crisis intervention, counseling, de-escalation, case -management. I was well-versed in reading people and situations. I knew how to establish rapport and to connect.

As individuals, we all have an inherent need for connection. The benefits of connection are innumerable. I chose social work so I could connect with and help others. I felt confident in my skills and abilities. Until, I didn't.

How does one connect with an individual who is only alert and oriented to him/herself? I felt helpless, questioning my decision to work in hospice. That is, until that day, during my fourth week as a Hospice Social Worker.

I was making a routine visit at a Skilled Nursing Facility. I approached my patient as she was sitting in her wheelchair, in the main living area. I sat next to her and said her name. She looked at me, and resumed staring ahead. I held her hand and spoke words of affirmation. She continued to stare ahead.

I glanced over my shoulder to the large bookcase filled with volumes of books. I walked over and pulled out a book - an encyclopedia of insects. Placing the book gently on her lap, I turned each page. I commented on the colors and the "ickiness" of several of the bugs. She began to also remark on the "ick" and the colors, too.

Our entire life journey is about connection. The bonds we build with others. Finding the beauty in everyone and everything. And, expressing love and compassion.

My wish for you is that you are able to use this book as a tool to connect with your loved ones and patients. And find comfort in doing so.

The Colors Within

The sun is going down and the air
is becoming cooler.
The Kaleidoscope of colors
slowly fade, replaced by a dark canvas
with sparkling diamonds.
Holding back tears, I think of you.
Your bright, colorful persona
ebbing away like timeworned photographs.
Curious eyes, now vacant, lost.
Your comforting presence, now
timid and unassuming.
The brilliant palette void of
pigment.
Tears falling, I remember
your colors within.
Those beautiful magical
colors within.

Dedicated to JV
and all individuals and their families
affected by dementia.

This Moment

This is a moment in time.
It is in each moment of every day
where we truly experience life.
This moment is now. Not the past. Not the future. Now.
We breathe and live in this moment. Now.
Live each day with intention, purpose, and acute awareness.
Embrace this moment. Now.
This moment.

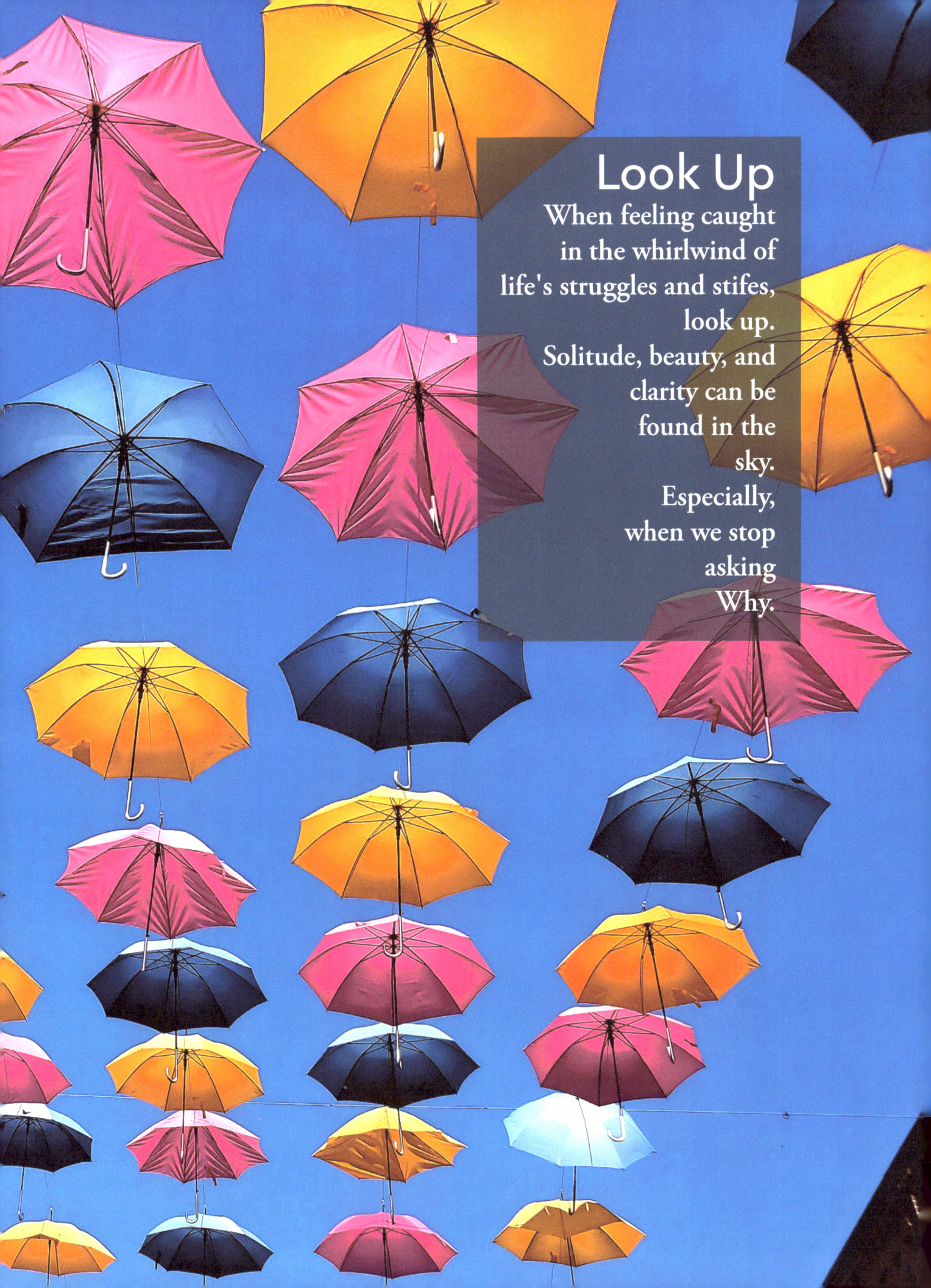

Look Up
When feeling caught in the whirlwind of life's struggles and stifes, look up. Solitude, beauty, and clarity can be found in the sky. Especially, when we stop asking Why.

Time

They say time heals all things, I wonder if this so. The grief I hold within my heart; penetrates my soul. I grieve for all I have lost and what will never be. I yearn for a future with shared memories. Tears are a fuel for strength; I succumb, and then I rest. I will love you forever. Even after my last breath.

Change
Life is a
continuous cycle.
There is a
beginning, an end,
and
hardship, growth,
and beauty
inbetween.
Just as seasons
change,
the difficult times in
our lives give way
to better days,
Life may not get
easier; we do get
stronger.
The only constant
 in life is change.
Letting go and
accepting
change.

"But those who HOPE in the Lord will renew their STRENGTH.

They will fly as high as EAGLES. They shall run and not be weary, they shall walk and not get tired."

Isaiah 40:31

Fragments

Old photographs are
emotional artifacts.
preserving moments
of time. Mirrorring,
reminding us
who we are
where we came from
why we are here.
Narrating, evoking,
emoting.
Fragments of what was.

MARINETTE

Bridges
Bridges.
Connecting past, present
and future.
Memories, experience,
hopes and dreams.
They meld together
at one point
in time.
A time encapsulated
in our hearts.
Forever.

Life's Roads

Life rarely follows a
straight path.
The bends in the road,
life's challenges,
give way to beauty.
Each curve,
each defining moment,
shape us
and our journey.
Hidden views
guide us to
an understanding which
emerges
over time.

Storms
Chaotic, Unpredictable. They can uproot even the strongest tree and unsettle the seasoned sailor. Yet, in the midst of life's storms, there's always the possibility of a calm renewal. Transformation Yielding clarity And Hope.

Pristine Imperfection, Old dwellings shelter and protect. A testament to the endurance and passage of time. Despite the elements and hardships, strength and beauty remain untouched. Just as you and I will weather the frailty of life's encounters.

"How many are your works, Lord! In wisdom, you made them all: The earth is full of your creatures. There is the sea, vast and spacious, teeming with creatures beyond number living things both large and small."

Psalm 104:24-25

Autumn
A time of change.
A time to let go of
Expectations and
what no longer serves us.
A time for shedding life's hurts.
Transitional transformation.
Anticipating and
preparing for what
lies ahead.
A time for gathering wisdom
and strength.

Polished Rocks

Like polished rocks
with their ornate
sculpted beauty, crafted by
pressure and time,
we, too, are shaped by
life's experiences.
A culmination of everything
that once was.
And like the hardened stones,
We endure and defy.
Facing tomorrow with
grace and fortitude.

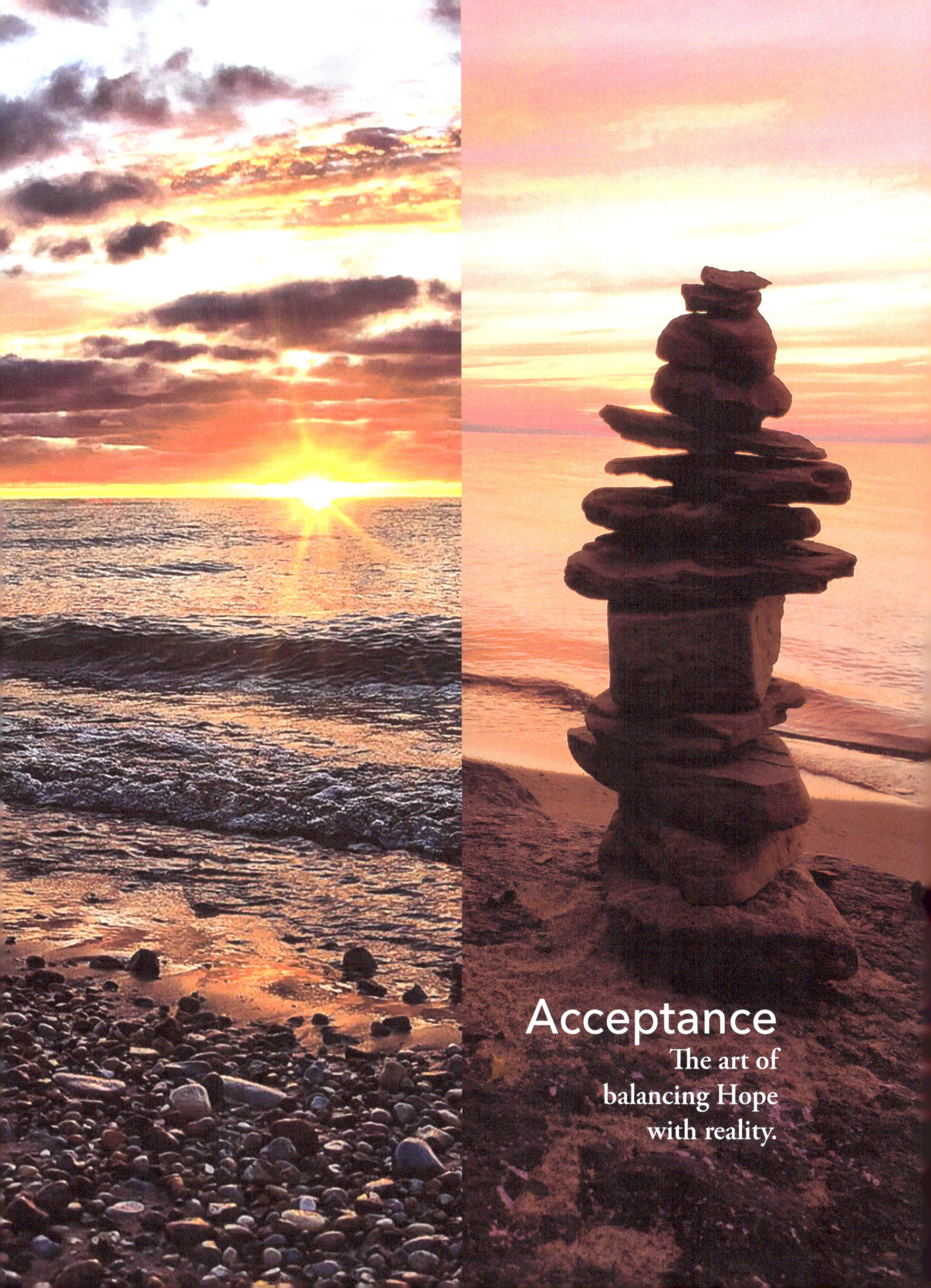

Acceptance
The art of balancing Hope with reality.

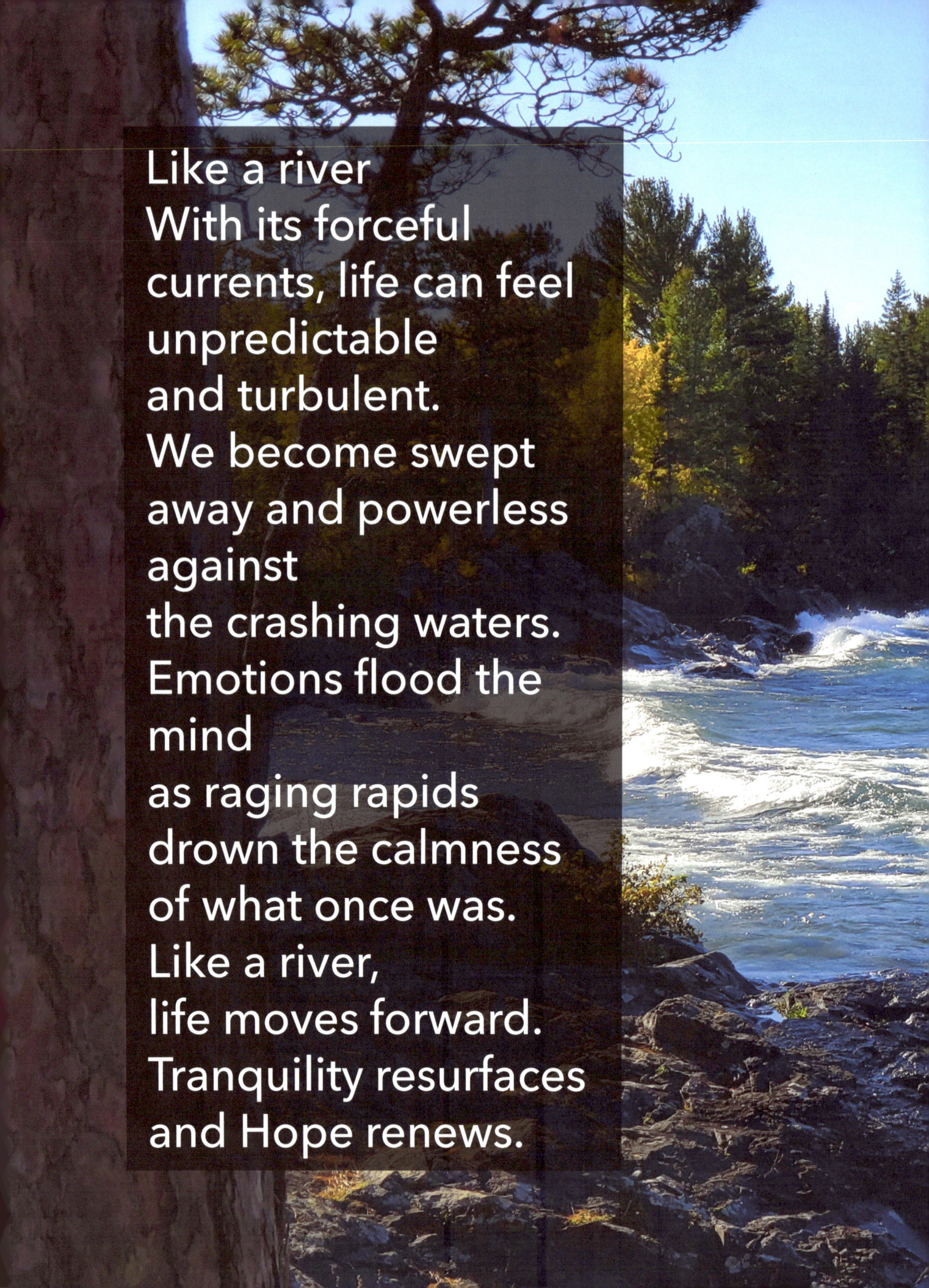

Like a river
With its forceful
currents, life can feel
unpredictable
and turbulent.
We become swept
away and powerless
against
the crashing waters.
Emotions flood the
mind
as raging rapids
drown the calmness
of what once was.
Like a river,
life moves forward.
Tranquility resurfaces
and Hope renews.

Snow Covered Bridges

A traveler must cross
a snow-covered bridge
with attention
and care.
Moving forward
despite ambiguity.
Like the traveler, life beckons
us to continue through
difficult times and
adversity.
The road ahead
may be covered
in uncertainty.
A passage
which requires
vigilance,
faith and
courage.
To be requited and restored
on the other
side.

Experience the Seasons

Seek beauty in each day
anticipating hidden
treasures.
Experience the seasons
celebrating life's pleasures.

To deny hurt and loss
is an unspoken travesty.
To heal, one must feel;
love abundantly.

Look towards the Heavens,
for wisdom, for strength.
Experience the seasons,
Experience God's grace.

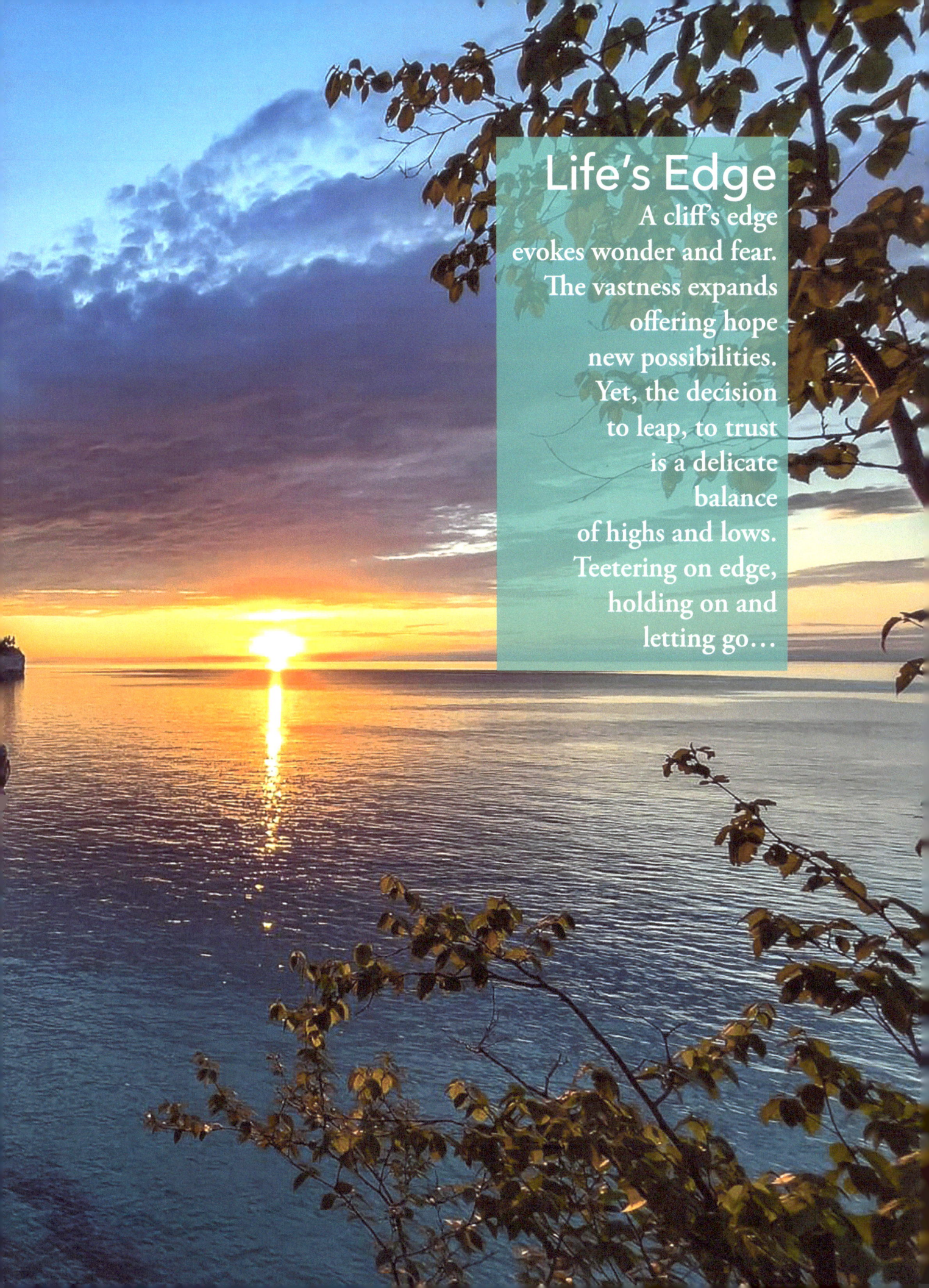

Life's Edge

A cliff's edge
evokes wonder and fear.
The vastness expands
offering hope
new possibilities.
Yet, the decision
to leap, to trust
is a delicate
balance
of highs and lows.
Teetering on edge,
holding on and
letting go…

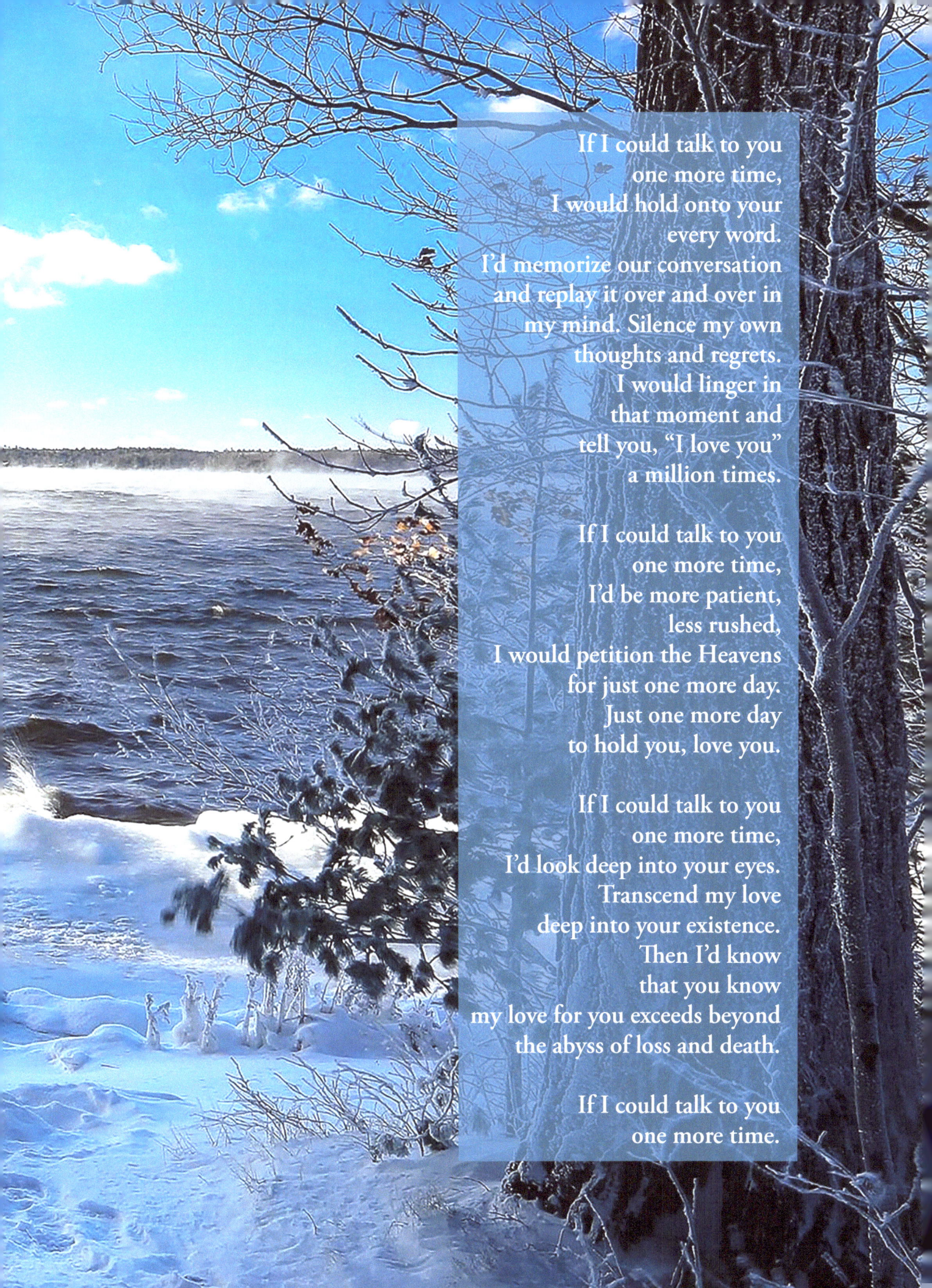

If I could talk to you
one more time,
I would hold onto your
every word.
I'd memorize our conversation
and replay it over and over in
my mind. Silence my own
thoughts and regrets.
I would linger in
that moment and
tell you, "I love you"
a million times.

If I could talk to you
one more time,
I'd be more patient,
less rushed,
I would petition the Heavens
for just one more day.
Just one more day
to hold you, love you.

If I could talk to you
one more time,
I'd look deep into your eyes.
Transcend my love
deep into your existence.
Then I'd know
that you know
my love for you exceeds beyond
the abyss of loss and death.

If I could talk to you
one more time.

Acceptance

To experience peace
we must accept what we
can not change.
Peace is not the absence of
troubles, challenges.
Peace entails acquiescing
reality without blame.
Navigating the
uncertainties
with grace.
In turn, we are able to
fully immerse in love
from a place of
understanding,
compassion, and
strength.

"Even though I walk through the valley of death, I will fear no evil, for you are with me: your rod and your staff, they comfort me."

Psalm 23:4

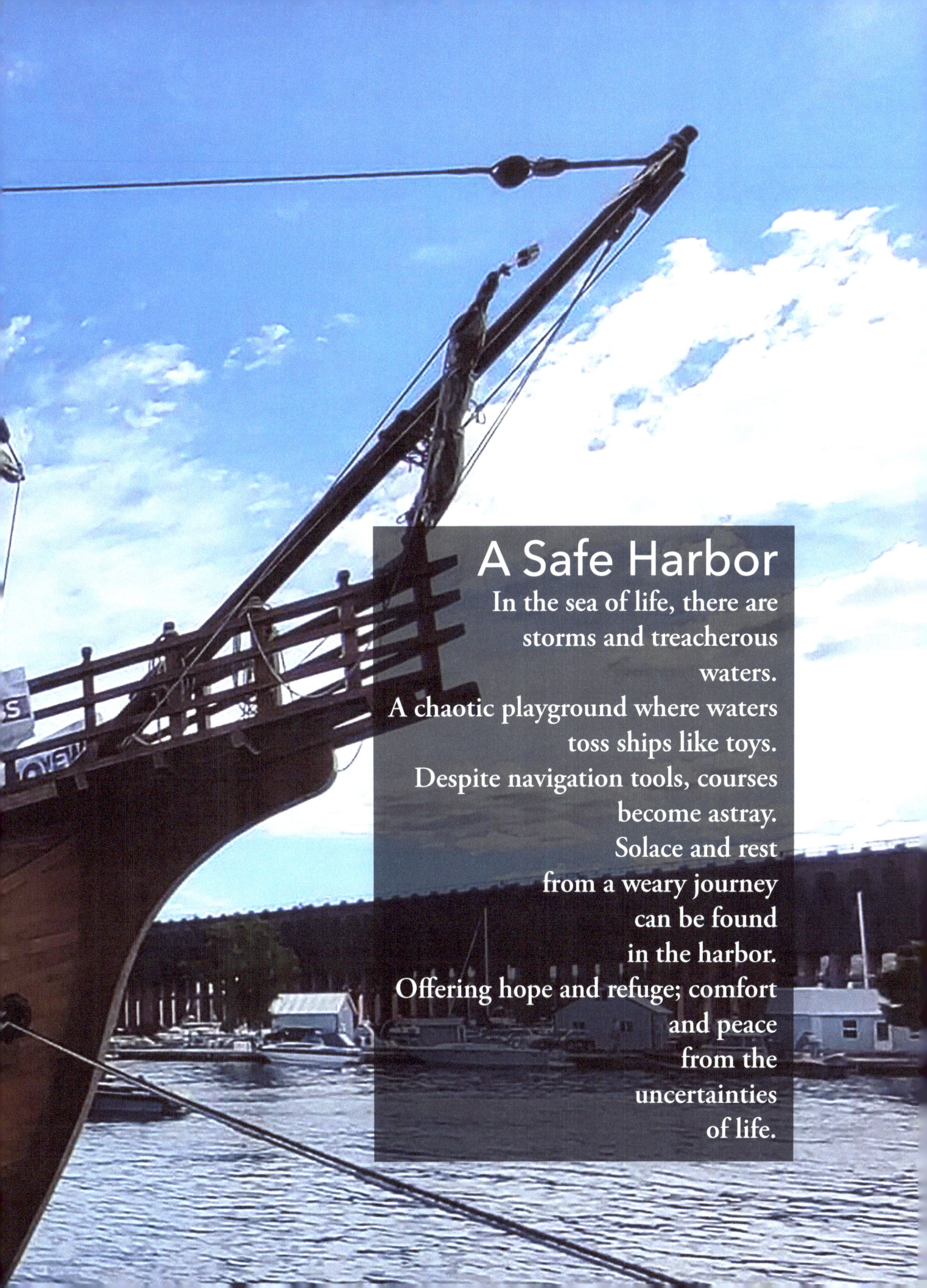

A Safe Harbor

In the sea of life, there are storms and treacherous waters.
A chaotic playground where waters toss ships like toys.
Despite navigation tools, courses become astray.
Solace and rest from a weary journey can be found in the harbor.
Offering hope and refuge; comfort and peace from the uncertainties of life.

Untitled

The chambers of my mind echo loudly.
Thoughts, fears, memories, all fight for attention.
Raging ruminations.
I close my eyes, and I render to a time where roles were reversed.
You're hold me, saying, "Everything is going to be okay."
Now, with more confidence than I feel, I say, "Everything is going to be okay. Everything, is going to be okay."

Northern Lights

Life's fleeting extraordinary moments. A natural light display caused by disturbances. An admonition to embrace the present moment, and to appreciate the vastness of life. Earth's reminder that there is beauty in the darkness.

Fly High

The connection and unity
birds
display in the air
is harmonious, numinous.
Wings spread,
attesting an open ease
in which they soar
through life.
Collective strength
exemplified through
formation.

We are similar to
our feathered friends.
To aviate long distances,
we, also, can not do it
alone.
We require others
to guide us,
to lift us up.
No one flies solo
through life.

Fields of Growth

Life's labor
yields moments of
drought, growth, and glory.
Seasons of effort
and reward
balanced
by dormancy.
Crops grow strong and tall,
as we, too, weather
life's elements and endure
junctures and circumstance.
Surviving, thriving;
living and dying.
Saying goodbye to
Summer's end;
the fields of growth
abiding.

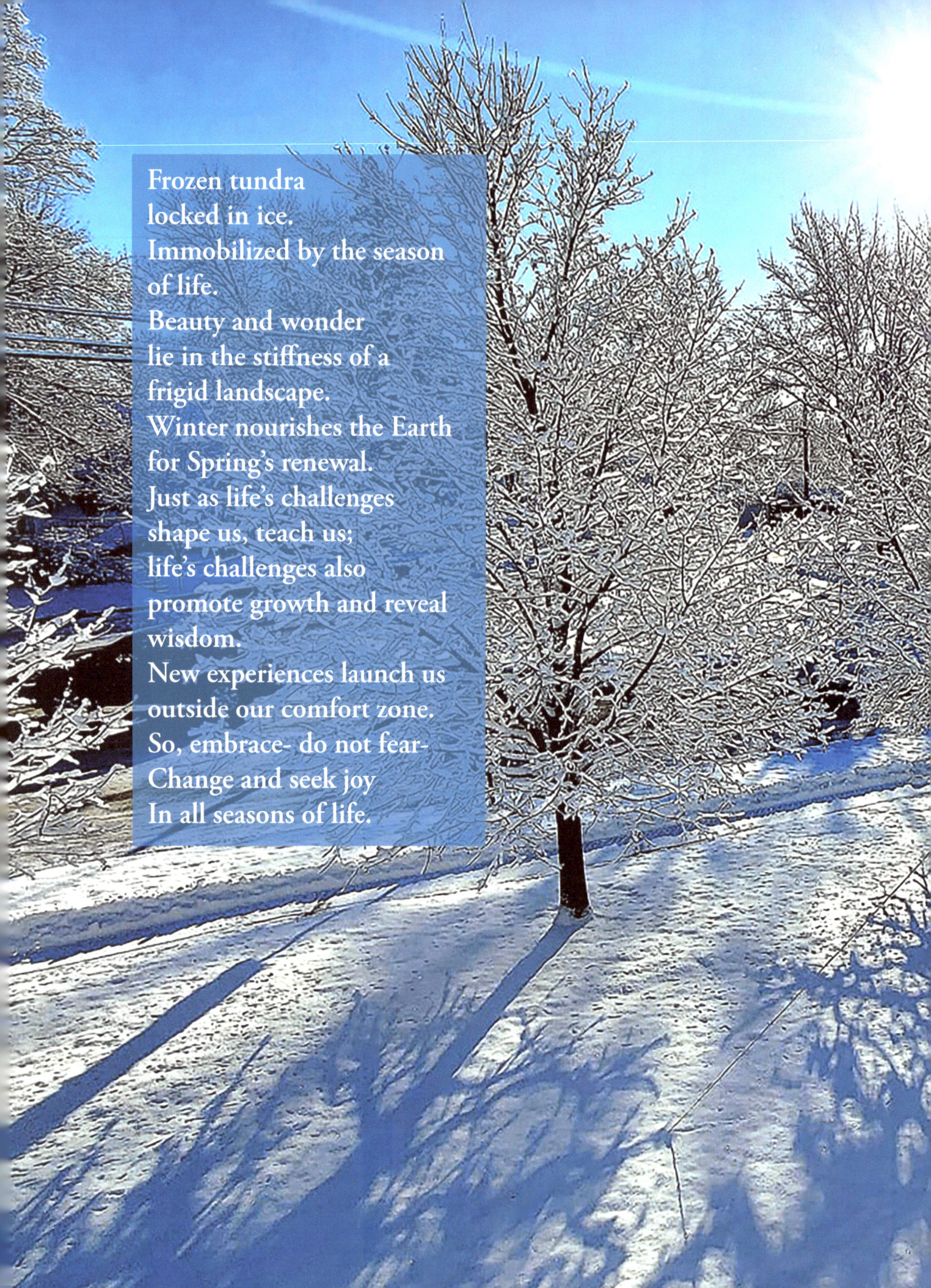

Frozen tundra
locked in ice.
Immobilized by the season
of life.
Beauty and wonder
lie in the stiffness of a
frigid landscape.
Winter nourishes the Earth
for Spring's renewal.
Just as life's challenges
shape us, teach us;
life's challenges also
promote growth and reveal
wisdom.
New experiences launch us
outside our comfort zone.
So, embrace- do not fear-
Change and seek joy
In all seasons of life.

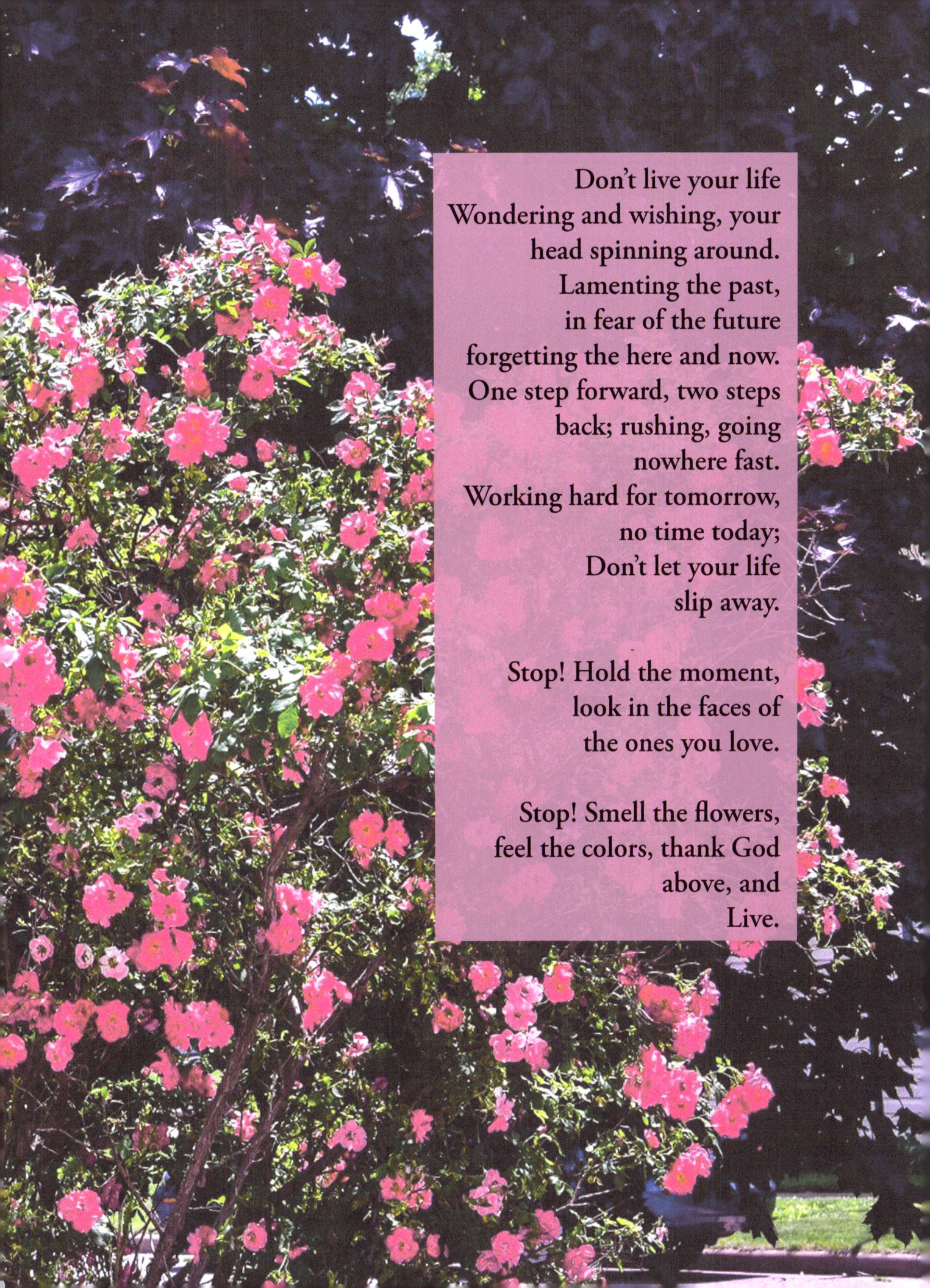

Don't live your life
Wondering and wishing, your
head spinning around.
Lamenting the past,
in fear of the future
forgetting the here and now.
One step forward, two steps
back; rushing, going
nowhere fast.
Working hard for tomorrow,
no time today;
Don't let your life
slip away.

Stop! Hold the moment,
look in the faces of
the ones you love.

Stop! Smell the flowers,
feel the colors, thank God
above, and
Live.

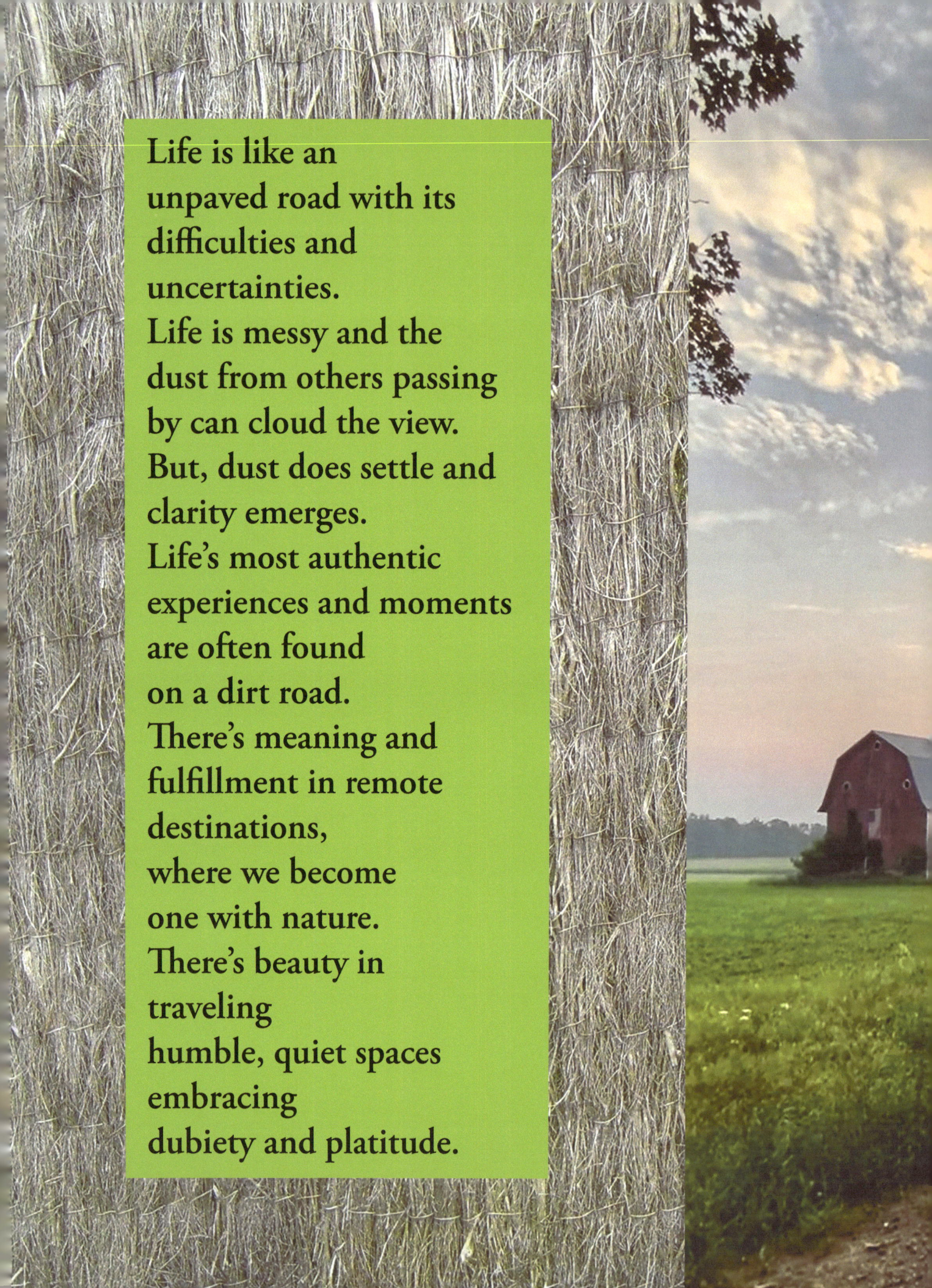

Life is like an
unpaved road with its
difficulties and
uncertainties.
Life is messy and the
dust from others passing
by can cloud the view.
But, dust does settle and
clarity emerges.
Life's most authentic
experiences and moments
are often found
on a dirt road.
There's meaning and
fulfillment in remote
destinations,
where we become
one with nature.
There's beauty in
traveling
humble, quiet spaces
embracing
dubiety and platitude.

A New Day

We may never
understand Why.
Question His plan.
Even doubt our Faith.
Waves of grief seize
our entire being,
exposing vulnerability
and brokenness.

We can resist what is-
Or- accept.
It is in acceptance where
we find peace.
And in peace, unearth
compassion, resilience.
The resilience to begin
A New Day.

Symbolically, the snowy owl is associated with purity, peace, honesty. Viewed as messengers or spiritual guides, they represent adaptability and wisdom. They remind us there is beauty, even in harsh environments. My message to you is this: Continue to love with wild abandonment and unconditional regard. Continue to focus on the present moment- this is where you will find joy. Continue to find comfort in treasured memories. And, continue to experience peace and anticipate Hope.

www.ingramcontent.com/pod-product-compliance
Lightning Source LLC
Chambersburg PA
CBHW041601070526
44586CB00003BA/44